THE BOOK
• OF •
AFFIRMATIONS

Self Love

by
TONYA TKO

HOW TO USE
THE BOOK OF AFFIRMATIONS
Self Love

This is a life-changing tool made of affirmations specially-crafted by a Certified Clinical Hypnotherapist to rewrite your subconscious programming. The first thing to remember is that this is YOUR book, you own it, so write in it, scribble on it and draw along it. This affirmations book is all about self love, so know that you are worth making this book your unique creation. There are no mistakes, so scribble away!

Half-hour before sleep your brain enters theta state and suggestions have an easier time penetrating into your subconscious mind. Choose any 2 pages and re-write the affirmations in the space provided. Write it word-for-word, (or substitute a word which resonates more with your particular tastes). Use the workbook pages to expound on your thoughts. Use additional pages/journals as needed.

It is important that you Physically write the sentences.

Write it, feel it, then go to sleep.
Repeat each night.
Watch the magic unfold.
GO TO WWW.SELFLOVEWORKBOOK.COM FOR BONUSES

♡
Tonya

My Life Matters
MY PRESENCE ON EARTH MATTERS

My Life Matters. My Presence on Earth Matters.
(Re-Write Affirmation Below)

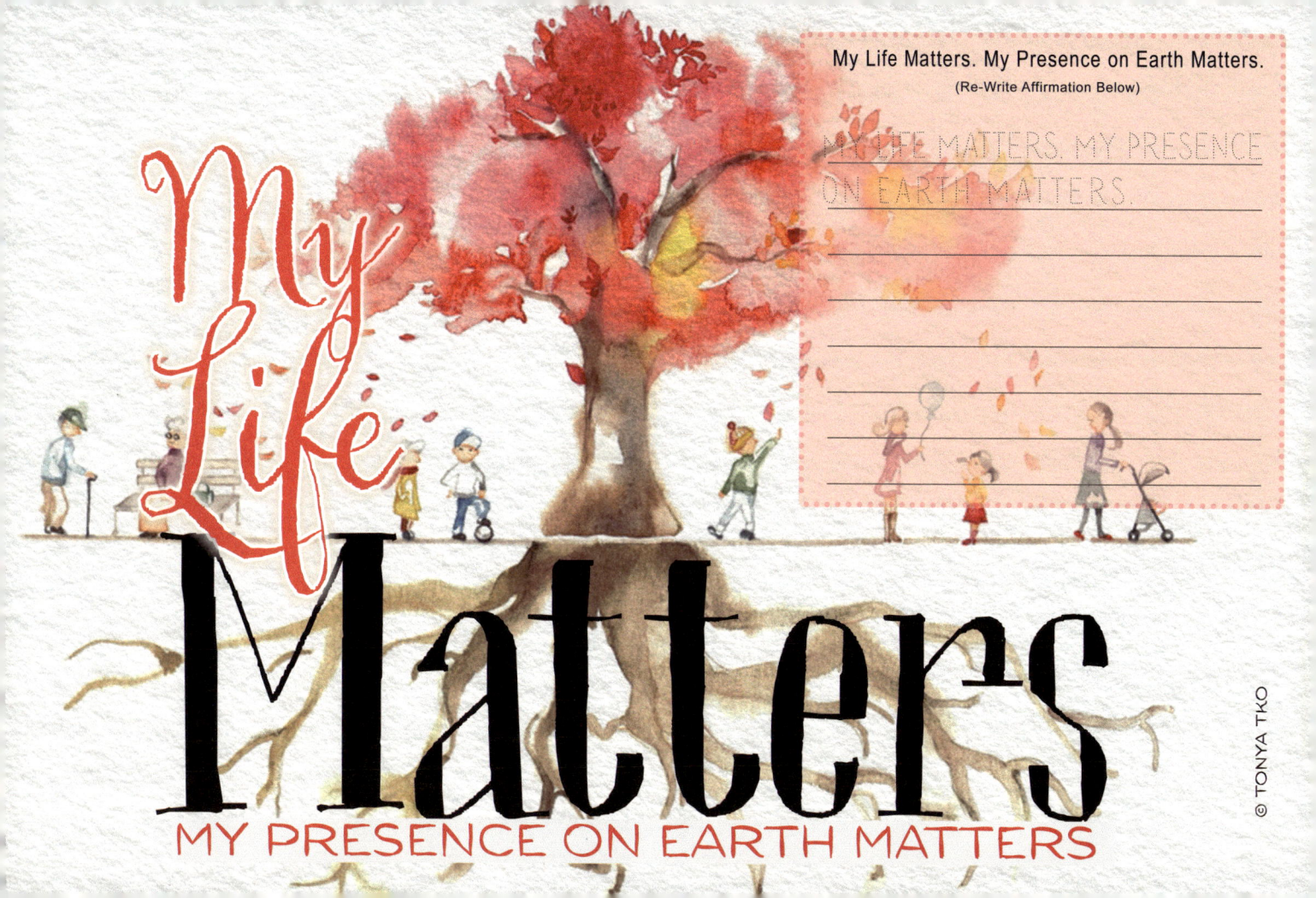

MY LIFE MATTERS. MY PRESENCE ON EARTH MATTERS.

© TONYA TKO

I Am a Seed with all of the Genetic Coding of a Mighty Tree

I Am a Seed with all of the Genetic Coding of a Mighty Tree
(Re-write affirmation below).

I AM A SEED WITH ALL OF THE
GENETIC CODING OF A MIGHTY TREE

_____
_____
_____
_____
_____
_____
_____
_____

© TONYA TKO

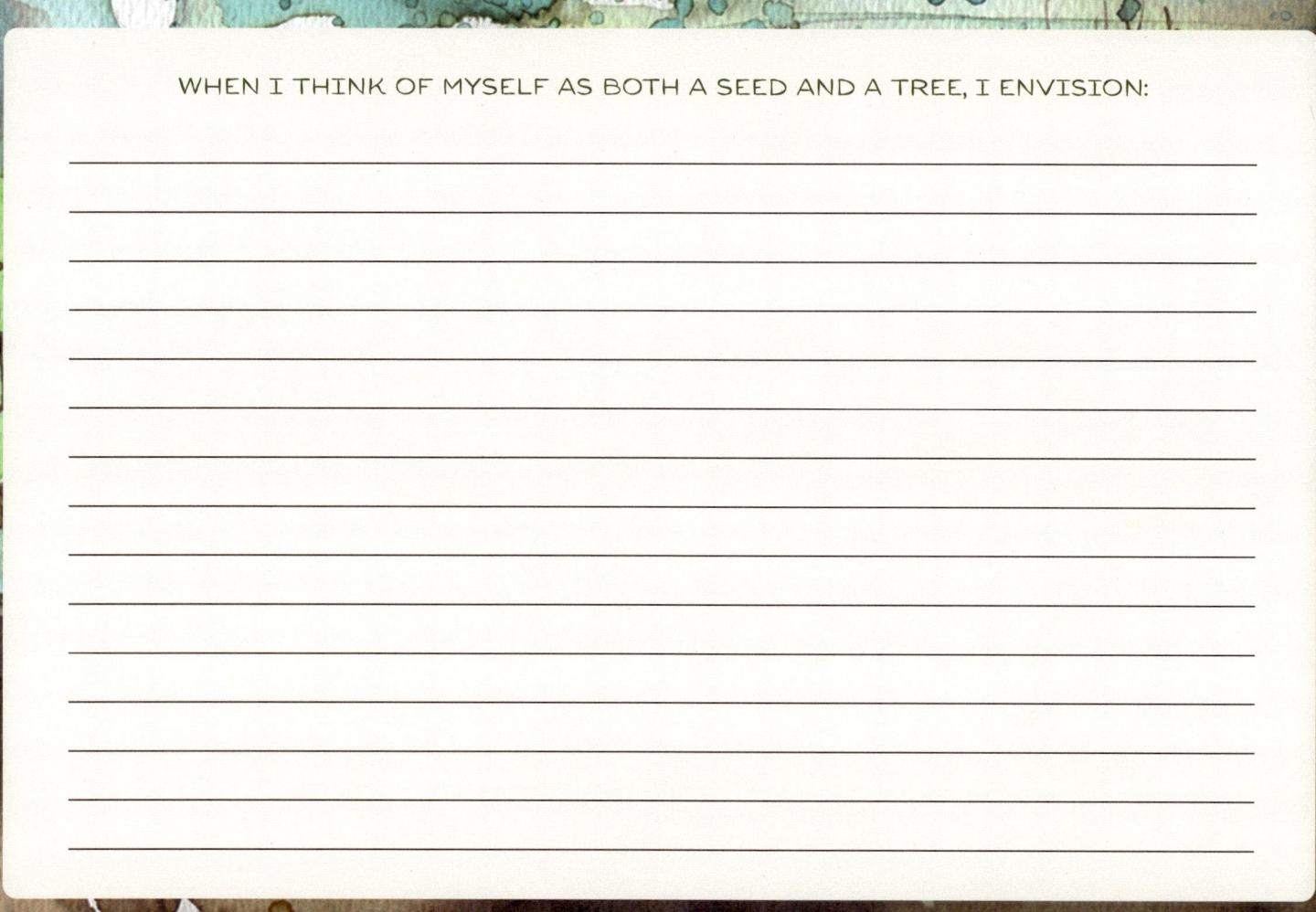

WHEN I THINK OF MYSELF AS BOTH A SEED AND A TREE, I ENVISION:

I AM STILL Writing My Story

© TONYA TKO

I Am Still Writing My Story
(Re-write affirmation below)
I AM STILL WRITING MY STORY

WRITE YOUR EULOGY
(IMAGINE WHAT A LOVED-ONE WOULD SAY & WRITE IT BELOW):

I Share My Gifts with Love & Ease

I Share My Gifts With Love & Ease
(Re-Write Affirmation Below)

I SHARE MY GIFTS WITH LOVE & EASE

I AM A GREAT PERSON. People love Me!

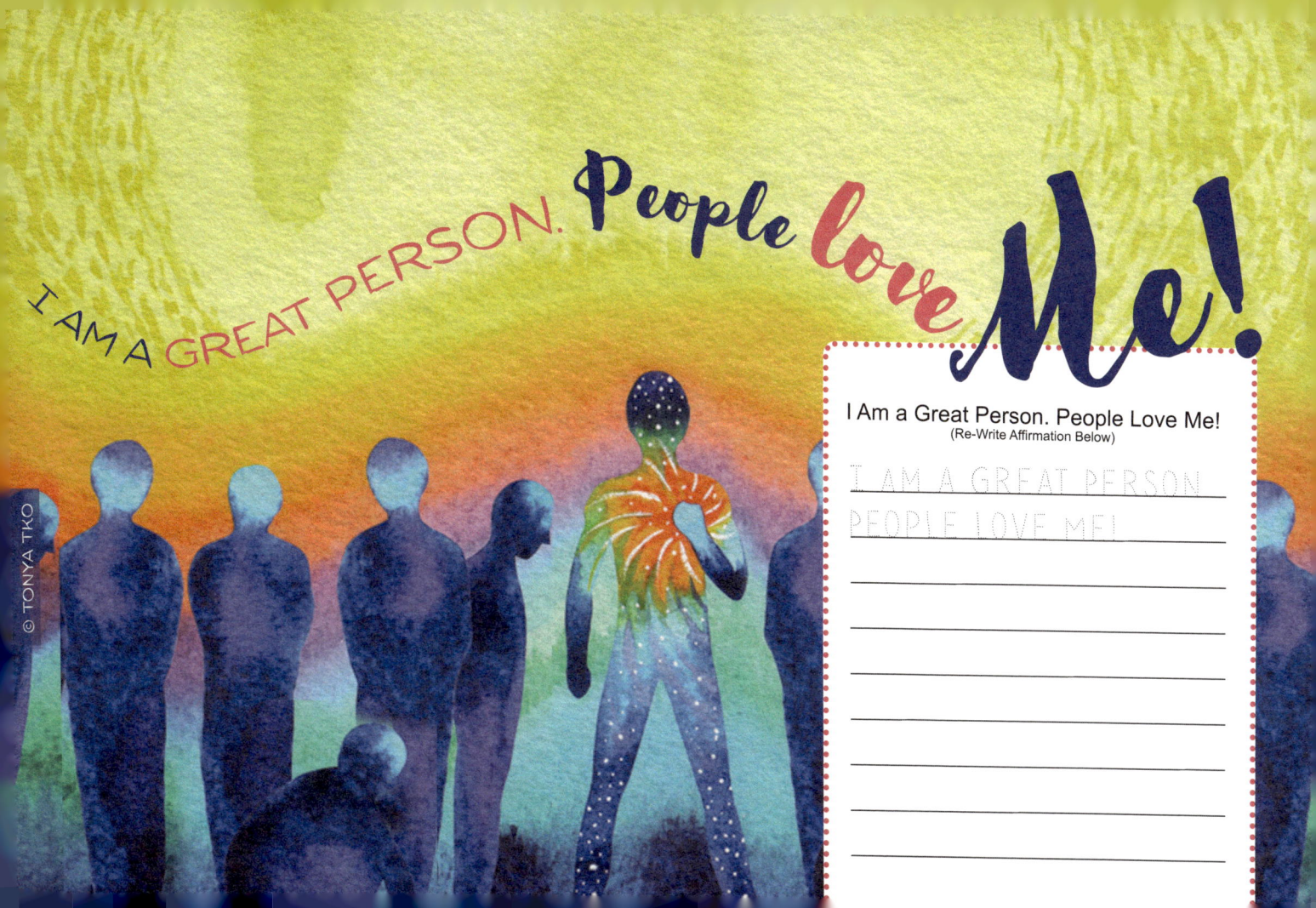

I Am a Great Person. People Love Me!
(Re-Write Affirmation Below)

I AM A GREAT PERSON
PEOPLE LOVE ME!

Every Step Is the Right Step

I TRUST

**Every Step Is the Right Step.
I Trust The Process.**
(Re-Write Affirmation Below)

EVERY STEP IS THE RIGHT STEP.
I TRUST THE PROCESS.

THE PROCESS

Each Step Brings Me Closer

**Each Step Brings Me Closer.
The Process, I Trust.**
(Re-Write Affirmation Below)

EACH STEP BRINGS ME CLOSER.
THE PROCESS, I TRUST.

© TONYA TKO

ENVISION A FUTURE GOAL. WORKING BACKWARDS, FIVE TO TEN STEPS I NEED TO TAKE ARE: (WRITE FUTURE DATE & WORK BACKWARDS 'TIL TODAY)

THE PREVIOUS PAGE PROJECTED INTO THE FUTURE. NOW, FOCUSING ON THE PRESENT, MY NEXT STEP IS:

I AM WORTHY of *Love* & Affection

I Am Worthy of Love and Affection.
(Re-Write Affirmation Below)

I AM WORTHY OF LOVE & AFFECTION

© TONYA TKO

I Am A Beautiful Flower
People Gravitate to Me
(Re-Write Affirmation Below)

I AM A BEAUTIFUL FLOWER
PEOPLE GRAVITATE TO ME

I AM A FORCE!

I AM A FORCE!
(Re-Write Affirmation Below)

I AM A FORCE!

© TONYA TKO

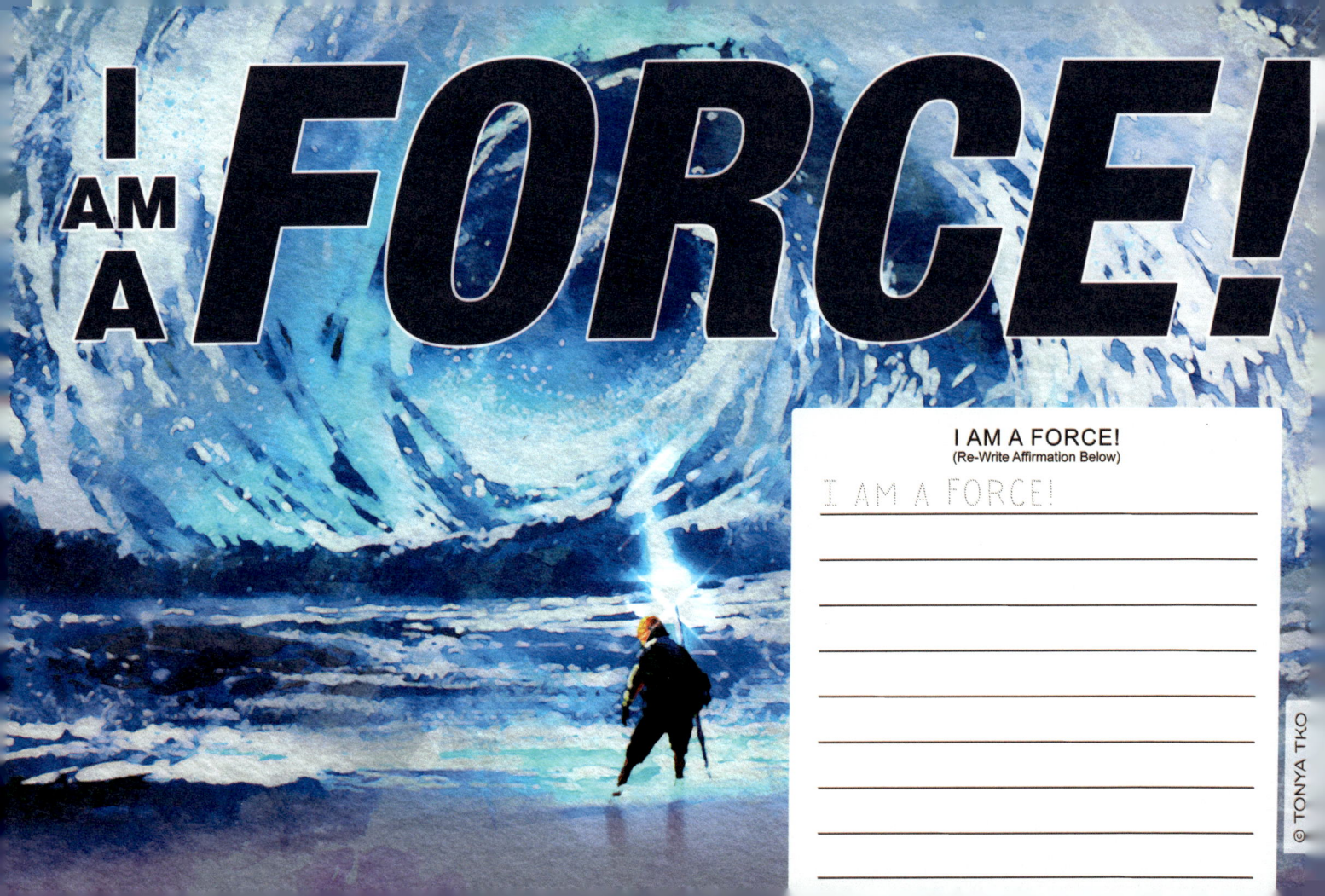

WHEN I ENVISION BEING A FORCE, I SEE (DESCRIBE IN DETAIL):

I LOVE MY BODY

I Love My Body. I Take Care of My Body. My Body Takes Care of Me!

(Re-Write Affirmation Below)

I LOVE MY BODY. I TAKE CARE OF MY BODY. MY BODY TAKES CARE OF ME!

I TAKE CARE OF MY BODY. My Body Takes Care of Me!

I Am Healthy Happy & Whole

(Re-Write Affirmation Below)

I AM HEALTHY HAPPY & WHOLE

I Am Healthy, Happy, & Whole

I AM A MAGNET For Love

ENDLESS LOVE FLOWS TO ME

I Am A Magnet For Love. Endless Love Flows To Me
(Re-Write Affirmation Below)

I AM A MAGNET FOR LOVE.
ENDLESS LOVE FLOWS TO ME

THE UNIVERSE
IS ON MY SIDE

It Conspires to Fulfill My Wishes

The Universe Is On My Side.
It Conspires to Fulfill My Wishes.
(Re-Write Affirmation Below)

THE UNIVERSE IS ON MY SIDE. IT CONSPIRES TO FULFILL MY WISHES.

© TONYA TKO

EACH AND EVERY DAY MORE & MORE **Abundance Flows My Way**

Each and Every Day, More & More Abundance Flows My Way
(Re-Write Affirmation Below)

EACH AND EVERY DAY MORE &
MORE ABUNDANCE FLOWS MY WAY

My Thoughts Support Me and Propel Me to My Highest Version

(Re-Write Affirmation Below)

MY THOUGHTS SUPPORT
ME AND PROPEL ME TO
MY HIGHEST VERSION

My Thoughts Support Me & Propel Me To My Highest Version

DESCRIBE IN DETAIL A TIME I FELT POWERFUL BEYOND MEASURE
(OR WHAT IT WILL LOOK LIKE WHEN I DO):

I AM POWERFUL *Beyond Measure!*

I AM POWERFUL BEYOND MEASURE.
(Re-Write Affirmation Below)

I AM POWERFUL BEYOND MEASURE.

© TONYA TKO

© TONYA TKO

TIME IS *an illusion*

There is more than enough time to accomplish everything

There is More Than Enough Time To Accomplish Everything. Time Is An Illusion.
(Re-Write The Affirmation Below)

THERE IS MORE THAN ENOUGH TIME TO ACCOMPLISH EVERYTHING TIME IS AN ILLUSION

HERE'S A LIST OF THE THINGS I'D DO WITH ALL THE TIME IN THE WORLD...

(THEN, START THE FIRST ITEM ON THE LIST TODAY... AND CONTINUE...)

I STAND MY GROUND with Love & Ease

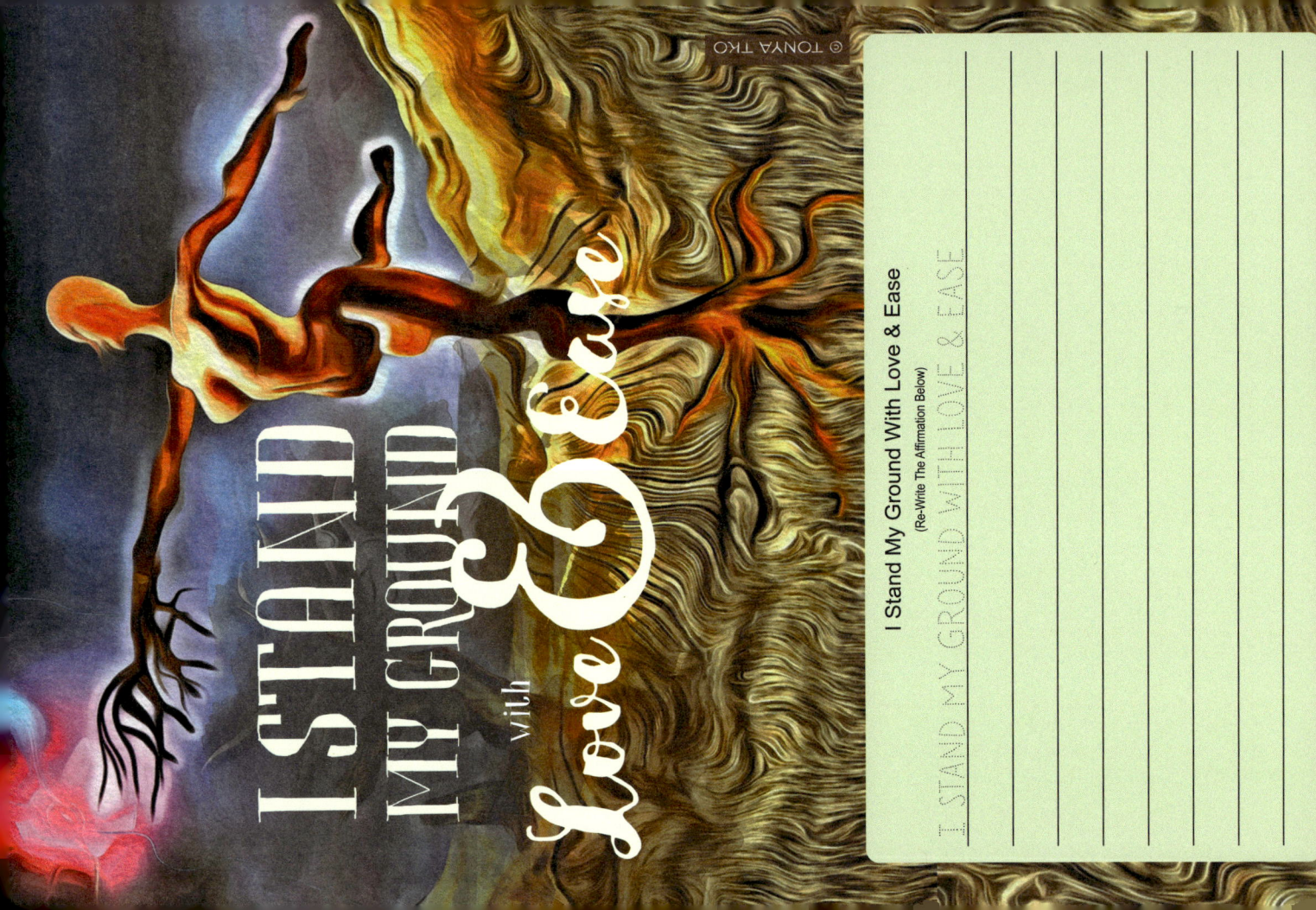

© TONYA TKO

I Stand My Ground With Love & Ease
(Re-Write The Affirmation Below)

I STAND MY GROUND WITH LOVE & EASE

THESE ARE MY BOUNDARIES
(AND THE HEALTHY CONSEQUENCES I IMPOSE IF THEY'RE CROSSED):

_____
_____
_____
_____
_____
_____
_____
_____
_____
_____
_____
_____
_____
_____
_____
_____
_____
_____
_____
_____
_____

I Deserve Rest & Relaxation

I DESERVE REST & RELAXATION
(Re-Write The Affirmation Below)

I DESERVE REST & RELAXATION
_____
_____
_____
_____
_____
_____
_____
_____

THE LEISURELY ACTS OF SELF-CARE I ENJOY ARE:

I AM WORTHY OF GREATNESS

Great Things Come To Me With Ease

© TONYA TKO

**I Am Worthy of Greatness,
Great Things Come To Me With Ease.**
(Re-Write The Affirmation Below)

I AM WORTHY OF GREATNESS.
GREAT THINGS COME TO ME
WITH EASE.

© TONYA TKO

I AM SAFE

I AM FOREVER PROTECTED & COVERED

I Am Forever Protected & Covered. I Am Safe.
(Re-Write The Affirmation Below)

I AM FOREVER PROTECTED & COVERED. I AM SAFE.

I AM THE MANIFESTATION OF AN ANCESTOR'S Dream

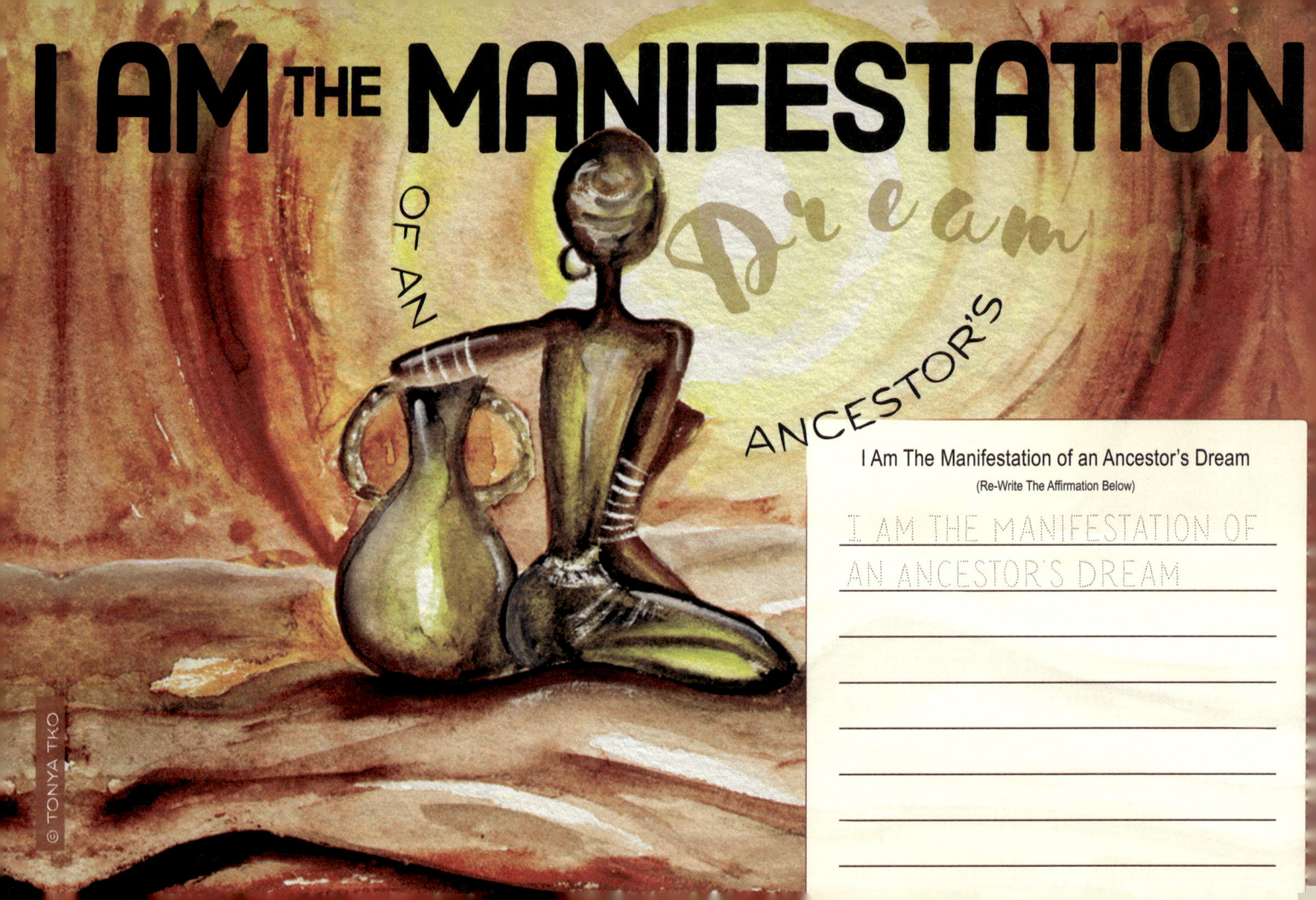

I Am The Manifestation of an Ancestor's Dream
(Re-Write The Affirmation Below)

I AM THE MANIFESTATION OF AN ANCESTOR'S DREAM
_____
_____
_____
_____
_____
_____
_____

SOME THINGS MY ANCESTORS DREAMED OF WHICH I CAN NOW DO/BE/HAVE:

_____
_____
_____
_____
_____
_____
_____
_____
_____
_____
_____
_____
_____

I AM Magnificent

© TONYA TKO

I Am Magnificent
(Re-Write The Affirmation Below)

I AM MAGNIFICENT

An Endless Supply of Love Surrounds Me

An Endless Supply of Love Surrounds Me
(Re-Write The Affirmation Below)

AN ENDLESS SUPPLY OF LOVE SURROUNDS ME

© TONYA TKO

It Takes Just One Moment to Change a Life
Life is Magical
It Takes Just One Moment to Change a Life
(Re-Write The Affirmation Below)
LIFE IS MAGICAL. IT TAKES
JUST ONE MOMENT TO CHANGE
A LIFE
LIFE IS MAGICAL
© TONYA TKO

DESCRIBE 3 TIMES SOMETHING SEEMINGLY SMALL HAD A LIFE-LONG POSITIVE IMPACT:

TIME IS an illusion

Time Is An Illusion*
(Re-Write The Affirmation Below)

TIME IS AN ILLUSION
_____
_____
_____
_____
_____
_____
_____

IMAGINE TIME IS ON A VERTICAL PLANE, WHAT IS YOUR FUTURE SELF DOING RIGHT NOW?: (WRITE YOUR FUTURE SELF A LETTER & WRITE A LETTER BACK FROM YOUR FUTURE SELF)

_____
_____
_____
_____
_____
_____
_____
_____
_____
_____
_____
_____

*(TIME BEING AN ILLUSION IS SUCH AN IMPORTANT CONCEPT I ADDED IT TO THE BOOK TWICE)

**TAKE A LOOK AROUND AND CHOOSE TO SEE THE MAGIC IN 3 THINGS.
(DESCRIBE WHAT YOU SEE/FEEL/SENSE): (GO OUTSIDE & REPEAT)**

_____
_____
_____
_____
_____
_____
_____
_____
_____
_____
_____
_____

I CHOOSE TO SEE THE MAGIC OF LIFE ALL AROUND ME

I Choose to See the Magic of Life All Around Me

(Re-Write The Affirmation Below)

I CHOOSE TO SEE THE
MAGIC OF LIFE ALL
AROUND ME

I MATTER
MY LIFE IS IMPORTANT

© TONYA TKO

I MATTER. MY LIFE IS IMPORTANT.
(Re-Write The Affirmation Below)

I MATTER. MY LIFE IS IMPORTANT.

I am Grateful for Life. Life is a Beautiful Gift!

I Am Grateful For Life.
Life is a Beautiful Gift.
(Re-Write The Affirmation Below)

I AM GRATEFUL FOR LIFE.
LIFE IS A BEAUTIFUL GIFT.

© TONYA TKO

KEEP MOVING.

Just Keep Putting One Foot In Front Of The Other

KEEP MOVING.
Just Keep Putting One Foot In Front of The Other

(Re-Write The Affirmation Below)

KEEP MOVING. JUST KEEP PUTTING ONE FOOT IN FRONT OF THE OTHER

© TONYA TKO

I DON'T NEED TO FOCUS ON THE ENTIRE JOURNEY, JUST THE NEXT STEP. MY NEXT STEP IS:

_____
_____
_____
_____
_____
_____
_____
_____
_____
_____
_____
_____

RE-WRITE ANY AFFIRMATION IN YOUR OWN WORDS:

_____
_____
_____
_____
_____
_____
_____

CREATE NEW AFFIRMATIONS WHICH RESONATE WITH YOU:

_____
_____
_____
_____
_____
_____
_____

NOTES

_____
_____
_____
_____
_____